HOW TO DEAL WITH DIFFICULT PEOPLE

Smart Tips on How to Handle the People Problem and Get the Best Out of Your life

© Written by:Katerina Griffith

Text Copyright © [Katerina Griffith]

Legal & Disclaimer

such other professional advisor) before using any of the suggested remedies, techniques, or information in this book.

Upon using the contents and information contained in this book, you agree to hold harmless the Author from and against any damages, costs, and expenses, including any legal fees potentially resulting from the application of any of the information provided by this book. This disclaimer applies to any loss, damages or injury caused by the use and application, whether directly or indirectly, of any advice or information presented, whether for breach of contract, tort, negligence, personal injury, criminal intent, or under any other cause of action.

You agree to accept all risks of using the information presented inside this book.

You agree that by continuing to read this book, where appropriate and/or necessary, you shall consult a professional (including but not limited to your doctor, attorney, or financial advisor or such other advisor as needed) before using any of the suggested remedies, techniques, or information in this book.

Table of Contents

Book Description

Have you ever encountered someone who is frustrating to the point you feel like pulling your hair? Has someone ever driven you so crazy that you feel like screaming out loud?

Look around you – there are people in your life that are difficult to work or deal with.

You are not alone!

One thing that I have encountered over the years is a fair share of difficult people – friends, family, and coworkers alike. These are people who don't bother to turn in their work within the agreed timelines, people who hold on tightly to their views that no one else's matter at all. People who do not want to collaborate with others in a team. Those who push back on work they are supposed to do in the first place – so much more!

Here, we will discuss;

- How to identify a difficult person: The big five
- Types of difficult people
- Common traits of difficult people
- Why you must deal with a difficult person
  o At the workplace
  o Home
- Identifying the issue
- Three lenses to look at the world
- How to manage your reactions
- Leveraging self-control
- Steps on how to deal with a difficult person
- What do you do when all this does not work?
- Expert techniques to handle difficult people
- Actionable Tips and Trick

So, what are you still waiting for? It is time to handle those difficult people in your life gracefully and survive the drama they attract.

Read on and find out more!

Introduction

Are there difficult people in your life? I guess that's why you are here. If you have not encountered difficult people before, then it is high time you start preparing for when that happens – because it will!

The thing with difficult people is that they often defy logic. Unfortunately, some of them are blissfully unaware of the kind of damage their attitude has on the people around them. Others are aware of the negative impact their actions cause but yet choose to derive their satisfaction from stirring up chaos and pushing people's buttons hard to know how far they can go. Whichever the case, their actions create unnecessary complexity, stress, and strife.

I run a business where we have over 200 employees. As we collaborate on various projects from time to time, there are instances where we encounter difficulties in getting a unanimous agreement on something because each member of the team is strongly opinionated. When I just started the company, I used to get bothered and so worked up in such situations. Each time I'd think, "Why are these people too difficult to deal with? What an irresponsible group...I don't even want to work with them anymore; I will fire them all!"

After some time, I realized that difficult people are everywhere. Even at home, I was dealing with a difficult teenage daughter who thought that she knew everything, and nothing you told her made any sense at all! The truth is, no matter where you are at or where you go, you will never be able to hide from such people. While it might be possible to avoid the first 1 or 2 of them, what of the 3rd, 5th, ...n^{th} ones out there that you have not met yet? Avoiding these people is not a permanent solution unless you are willing to quit your job or move away from your home and never have anyone around you.

I don't know about you – but I think that this is not possible! Instead of running each time and trying to find solace where you will never find it, why not learn some incredible skills that will help you survive difficult people with so much ease and grace?

According to research, it is evident that difficult people can cause those around them stress. What is even more disturbing is the fact that fear has been shown to have a lasting negative impact on the human brain. When you are exposed to stress even just for a few days, the effectiveness of the neurons in your hippocampus – the part of the brain that is responsible for memory and reason – becomes compromised. If the stress goes on for several months, then the neurons are likely to get damaged. In other words, anxiety is one of the formidable threats to achieving success. If it gets out of control, then the chances are that your performance is affected.

The good news is that some of the common

causes of stress are very easy to identify. For instance, if your company is working towards getting a grant for you to function, there is a high chance that you will feel stressed and learn how to manage it. However, when the source of stress is unexpected, then chances are that it will take you by surprise, and this is what causes the most harm.

According to research from the Department of Clinical and Biological Psychology, Friedrich Schiller University, and exposure to a stimulus that causes a negative emotion is the same as when one is exposed to difficult people. The two experiences cause one's brain to have a massive response to stress. In other words, when one is negative, crueler lazy, that alone is enough to drive the mind into a state of anxiety.

It is important to note that your ability to manage your emotional feelings and stay calm even when you are under so much pressure has a direct association with your performance. According to findings by TalentSmart, over 90% of top performers in any organization are skilled at managing their emotions during stress periods. What is interesting is that the reason why they have control over these stressful situations is that they have learned how to neutralize difficult people.

While there are several strategies I have learned over the years from some of the top performers – who are my role models – on how to effectively deal with difficult people, I choose to share them here with you. If you are going to deal with difficult people effectively, then you need an approach that cuts across the board to the things you can eliminate. What you need to understand henceforth is that you are in control of how you respond to different situations more than you can imagine. Take charge today with the following strategies, and your life and experiences with people will never be the same again!

Keep reading!

Chapter 1

How to identify a difficult person:

The big five

It is important to note that difficult people come in all forms and sizes. There is a wide range of ways in which difficulty can manifest itself. This can be someone spreading false rumors, seeing negativity in everything, lack of cooperation, and those who don't see value in others' contributions and views, among others. The thing with difficult people is that they see an opportunity to create trouble. They tend to use passive resistance to bring down your efforts to move your goals ahead.

Note that at the end of the day, the definition of 'difficult' is something rather peculiar to every individual. In other words, what you consider challenging to you may not be the same thing to someone else. Therefore, you must understand your personality, triggers, and preferences so that you are better placed to take note of situations and people that get on your nerves.

Emotional Stability

This is also referred to as neuroticism. You may be wondering what this is. Well, neuroticism is one of the factors that go a long way in determining one's level of emotional stability. How do you react or respond to a stimulus? If your score is high, then this indicates that you are no stranger to such emotional feelings as anger, anxiety, and depression. There is a high chance that you experience these emotions on an ongoing basis. In other words, if you score highly on neuroticism, this indicates that you are emotionally reactive as opposed to those who score lower.

The thing with emotional stability is that it indicates how prone you are too intense stimuli. However, what is important to note is that these emotional outbursts often tend to erode one's ability to think logically, make complex decisions, and cope with stress effectively. A high level of neuroticism manifests with a high level of negativity – which exacerbates the slightest setback resulting in one having a bad mood.

On the other hand, a low neuroticism level is indicative that you are emotionally stable. You are less prone to emotional outbursts and are calm. However, what you need to note is that having a lower level of neuroticism does not mean things will always be favorable on your part. Extroversion has a direct correlation with positivity. If you are going to deal with difficult people, then you have to learn how to break free from emotional setbacks.

Extraversion

The chances are that you are already aware of introvert-extrovert binary, right? What part of the scale do you fall? Well, one thing you need to note is that extraversion is a factor that determines how you interact with the world around you.

If you rank highly on the Extraversion scale, you are an extravert. The good thing with this trait is that you tend to possess a can-do it spirits. These are the kind of people who are always beaming with so much energy. They do well in social gatherings and when having physical experiences with the outside world.

On the other hand, are introverts. These are the ones that rank low on the Extraversion scale. An introvert is someone that is more laid back with a very minimal need for social interactions. While they are not so positive minded as the extraverts, the truth is that they are not depressed or shy, universally. However, you must note the fact that they find physical and social stimulations somewhat overwhelming. This explains the reason why prefer solitude – to process their emotions – but also a little bit of social intimacy.

Openness

Each one of us has a certain level of transparency. It is our level of openness to experience that goes a long way in determining how one embraces new ideas and experiences. When one is open to experience, they are said to be artistically curious, intellectual, and with a very keen sense of beauty. The good thing with openness to experience is the fact that people with this trait excel in creative roles often seen in people in the upper echelons of designs and academia. However, these kinds of people tend to stay away from tasks that require adherence to a set of guidelines, rules, and regulations.

Well, this is not to say that there are closed-minded people. The truth is that those who do not rank high on an openness to experience tests are often termed as "closed." These are the people who often have very few common interests to others. This explains why they tend to oppose ambiguity and subtlety – mostly in conversations fiercely – and do not respond well to change.

While people who are "Closed" don't often light the world with innovations, the truth is that they have superior roles and performances in such areas as police work and sales, among others – where protocols, rules, guidelines, and regulations are what takes precedence over all else.

Agreeableness

This is a measure of one's willingness and ability to engage with others in social events. While people tend to think that this trait is a universally beneficial feature from the outset, this is not always the case. Several people believe that agreeableness is something positive, but the truth is that just like all other traits, this also has its downsides. For instance, agreeable people are often racked with indecisiveness – especially when they are trying to complete high-stress or complex tasks.

The good thing with people with this trait is that they understand the importance of getting along with others. They hold a high consideration for others' emotions and goals – even higher than their interests. They are very friendly, relentless, helpful, and optimistic. To the onlookers, they are trustworthy and honest.

On the other end of the spectrum lie the disagreeable people - known to elevate their interests above anything else in this life. The thing with them is that they do not concern themselves with the wellbeing of those around them. Instead, they choose to pay attention to advancing their agendas and goals. Disagreeable people are very unfriendly, uncooperative, and does not give a rat's ass about anyone else. Such people are often found in science, business, military, among other professions.

Conscientiousness

This is a trait that measures the extent to which we can control our emotions. The truth is, our conscientiousness determines the scope of our success, possible experiences, and the best way to attain them.

According to research, there is evidence that shows that highly conscientious people often have been shown to have better control over their emotions. Even though such people tend to come off as dull and rigid, the truth is that they do well in whatever they put their minds to – with proper planning and motivation. The good thing is that they often try as much as they can to stay away from trouble and making erratic decisions. However, the problem arises when plans don't fall into place as anticipated or fail to meet their set high standards.

On the contrary, those who have low conscientiousness can delay their gratifications. This makes them more prone to adhering to their emotions. While this is something so much fun during parties and is something that people find valuable when situations arise, the problem is that they prove to be complicated. This explains the reason why they often get in trouble with people in authority.

That said, you may be wondering whether these big five traits are universal. According to a research study that looked into different people from over 50 cultural backgrounds, there is evidence that shows at least five dimensions can be used in accurately describing personality. This is the reason why several psychologists believe that the five personality dimensions are not just universal but also have a genetic link. According to David Buss, a psychologist, personality traits are a representation of the key characteristics that shape our social landscapes.

But what factors influence the big five personality traits?

According to research, it is evident that both environmental and biological factors go a long way in influencing and shaping our personality traits. Two studies suggest that both nurture and nature have a central role to play in personality development. One of the studies examined 123 pairs of identical twins and 127 of fraternal twins.

What was interesting was that 53% of the heritability pointed at extraversion, 44% conscientiousness, 41% each of neuroticism and agreeableness, and finally 61% for openness.

On the other hand, longitudinal studies suggest that the five personality traits tend to stabilize as one goes through from childhood to adulthood. According to one study involving working-age adults, there is evidence that personality traits stabilized over four years and very minimal change brought about by adverse life events.

Studies also show that maturation dramatically impacts the personality traits. As we progress in age, there is a tendency for one to become less extraverted, open, and neurotic. However, features like conscientiousness and agreeableness tend to increase with age.

That said, what is essential to bear in mind is that behavior is something that comes as a result of interaction between one's personality and other situational factors. The situation in which you find yourself in has a role to play in how you respond. However, these kinds of responses are consistent with one's personality traits.

Wrapping it up

The five personality traits that we have just discussed – extraversion, agreeableness, neuroticism, openness, and conscientiousness – account for the difference between people.

For instance, when researchers have studied the personality traits of such animals like chimpanzees and dogs, the same features are also observed, plus more. Take a minute to think about dogs, you know – keep at home or within your neighborhood. What you will notice is that they are different from each other. Some are more friendly, active, and outgoing than others. Some are emotionally stable, while others are not. Some are friendly and agreeable, while some are vicious.

The chances are that you already know dogs that are very conscientious than others – in other words, they try too hard to do what is required of them just so that their master is happy. On the other hand, you probably know other dogs who don't even care what their master wants. Dogs also vary in terms of how open they are to new experiences, while others are more explorative and curious.

The sixth personality that we do not have but animals have is the ability to be dominant while others are more submissive. While human beings differ in terms of dominance, humans are more reflective of extraversion than independent.

Several people wonder how possible it is just, to sum up, personality traits in only five features. Well, if you think of all the people you already know, you might realize that they differ much more than the five personality traits. However, take a minute to think of this; if you take one character at a time rather than a collective personality, you will start to appreciate how diverse we all are.

People differ in personality ranging from low to very high on each trait. Even though each of the personality traits involves a large number of possible scores along the spectrum, you can choose to simplify this by thinking of it on a scale of 5. Now, if someone scores from very low, moderately low, average, moderately high, to very high, this means that we can give each one a score between 1 and 5.

Now that we have five traits, each one of them has five possible score levels starting from very low to very high. If you do that, then you can get at least 3,125 possible combinations on all five traits. That means 5 x 5 x 5 x 5 x 5. This means that if you were to classify people into all possible unique combinations of the five big traits, you would have to use all the five levels of each trait.

Additionally, it is essential to note that based on one's standing, the traits will manifest in quite diverse ways. A character like neuroticism appears to be different based on where a person stands on that trait. Let us consider another simple example. If one is high in neuroticism and agreeableness, they will have more unpleasant emotions - even so, they are still pleasant to be around. In other words, the fact that they are neurotic means that they tend to be clingy, annoying but does not necessarily affect other people much. If that very person is highly neurotic but has low agreeableness, then you had better watch your back!

When someone is highly emotional and is disagreeable, the truth is that they will tend to make their problems your problems too. They will be very difficult to deal with. While neuroticism manifests itself in various ways depending on their level of agreeableness, what you need to note is that such combinations change how our behaviors manifest outwardly.

Chapter 2

Types of difficult people

Perfectionists

When I first started my company, it used to take me at least 12 hours to produce an article that I thought was worthy of being published. My writers would send in their work, and I spent sleepless nights trying to edit and come up with the "perfect" piece. The thing with a perfectionist personality is that nothing will ever be good enough. You will find ways to look for mistakes, even where there aren't any.

One thing that is important to note is that being a perfectionist is something that is crippling. There may be that person in the office that is so passionate about their work is bursting with ideas but unfortunately cannot express them with unbridled freedom. It is the same thing with perfectionism – it holds you back because of anxiety, a sense of haunting unfulfillment, and depression.

Well, so many people think that being a perfectionist is about harboring the desire to be perfect alone. The truth is that it goes beyond that. You are merely choosing to derive your self-worth from the world around you. That explains why you end up being overly sensitive to criticism or rejection, and you end up believing that you are a stupid worthless failure or bad.

If you are a people-pleaser, then that is a sign of being a perfectionist. The thing is, seeking perfection often causes people anxiety because all they are thinking of is how they can be the best. You desire to control the outcome of your actions just so that you can gain approval, acceptance, praise, and rewards.

But do you think that the perfectionist in your office knows that they are obsessive and cynical in their behaviors? Certainly not! Just like I was, they may not even know that they are perfectionists, let alone putting in efforts to stop.

So, how do you deal with them?

Well, the thing with a perfectionist is that they are often detail-oriented, negative towards others, and sticklers for the rules. If your boss, subordinate, or colleague is this kind of person, the ways to handle them vary widely.

Dealing with a perfectionist subordinate

There are different types of perfectionists based on the personality types that we have discussed in the previous chapter; neurotic perfectionist, narcissistic perfectionist, hyperattentive perfectionist, and the principled perfectionist. The thing that these people have in common is that they all notice details and have very high standards that an average person cannot even breath close. To deal with them, you must;

Avoid giving them large project scopes

One thing that is important to note is that most

perfectionists have admirable qualities that many people find worthy. However, there are quite a few of them who choose to hone skills on a small component of a project instead of paying attention to the bigger picture. If you work with these kinds of people, it is helpful to assign them to select tasks based on their skillset.

In other words, you can opt to give them projects that are limited in scope but are detail-oriented. The truth is that most of them are not willing to delegate tasks, and the best thing you can do is allow them to work on projects independently – as long as the project requires a unified vision to complete.

Appeal to their sense of vanity and empathy
What if your employee is a neurotic or narcissistic perfectionist? Well, these kinds of people have a powerful desire to please others. The most effective way to motivate them is to explain to them how their style of work affects those in the team. Ensure that you phrase it in

such a way that they realize you already know they have high standards – and that you appreciate these high standards they hold.

You may say things like, "Mary, you have very high standards, just like me. That is what this company is all about. However, remember that good morale is essential for good productivity." What you are merely telling them is that the best way forward is to give a compliment even where they feel like there is something to criticize.

Appeal to their self-interest

What you will note is that several perfectionists want to be so perfect – either because of internal or external motivation. If you find that a subordinate is treating their colleagues poorly in the workplace just because they are perfectionists, remind them that such kind of people struggles hard to climb up the ladder. Remind them that the more they raise the ranks, the more they have to learn how to compromise for the sake of the whole team. Say something like, "I know you have been trying to ensure details of the project have been attended to, and the book does everything. That is great because if one is going to get the big things right, they will have to start by getting the little ones right. You are on the right track to the big things. However, what you need to remember as you progress is that the upper rank is about looking at the bigger picture. This means that if you focus too hard on getting 100% success, that will only bog you down. Have a vision for the next phase and not just a tunnel vision that might cost you more than you can pay for."

When you put it like that, they will start to realize that 100% is not all that counts, but achieving the primary goal, however, the approach you take is what counts at the end of the day.

Dealing with a perfectionist colleague

Choose your battles wisely

When you are dealing with a perfectionist

colleague, it is paramount that you know when to take a stand and when to let go. While this is something difficult to attain, you must take time to think about how important the issue at hand is so that you know when the time is right to take a stand.

The first thing is for you to keep a perspective. Agreeing with what your boss says does not mean that you have to follow their suggestions to the letter. While this seems at first as being passive, simply say yes and move on with your life. This will reduce the chances of stirring up conflict and stress. Saying yes to what they say does not mean that you have given away your power. It is quite the opposite because this will set you free from paying attention to their demands.

Ask them what it is they would like to do differently

Did you know that criticism is one of the best ways perfectionists use to hide their insecurities? While this is upsetting, it always helps to remember that this is their defensive mechanism. They may just be lashing out because they feel insecure about one thing or the other.

When you take time to ask them what their preferred methods of going about something is, you are merely disarming those insecurities. Try telling them that you care about their emotions. When they realize that you understand their feelings, they will start to feel secure – and less critical in the future. Say things like, "I see that you are upset about the outcome of this project. Would you like a chance to talk about it?"

Stick to your guns

Think about it, is the issue you and your colleague have relevant? If so, then you are right to stick to your guns. There is a chance that no one at the office is aware that your colleague is a perfectionist. If there is something you consider relevant to you and disagree on, then realize that it is your right to spit it out.

Don't get me wrong- by disagreeing, I don't mean

that you should argue about it. Simply state what it is that you disagree with and then move on. You don't have to let that disagreement to define the kind of relationship you both have. Simply say things like, "I understand where you are coming from. I just think that our perspectives are quite different on this one."

If they stir up an argument, simply walk away. No one will blame you for walking away from a case.

Keep distance

One of the simplest ways you can stay away from conflict is keeping a safe distance from it. If you have to work together on a project, simply remind them that each one of you has their roles and responsibilities and that you will do yours to your supervisor's satisfaction and not theirs.

You always have the choice of disengaging. If they keep going on and on about inconsequential details, all you have to do is remain noncommittal. Simply make your escape with such statements as "Huh, I didn't know you felt that way."

Dealing with a perfectionist supervisor

Manage your manager

This is simply what I often refer to as 'managing up.' The main aim of doing this is to help you identify the personality of your boss – their strengths and weaknesses – so that you can effectively tailor your conversation to match theirs.

The problem with a perfectionist boss is that they always desire to be in charge. At first, this may be self-evident, but the truth is that it is not. Ask them what their expectations are. When you do this, you are giving them an enhanced feeling of being in control. This also protects you from providing an arbitrary response. While perfectionism may be unreasonable – inherently – you must try as much as possible not to be. The trick is for you to pay attention to their start points, endpoints, or boundaries to lower the chances of getting them angry.

Push information their way

Once you know what it is that your perfectionist boss is looking for, simply give them – don't wait until they ask for it. The more you offer them a wealth of information they are interested in, even before they can ask for it, the less likely they will think of you as a flawed person. This way, you escape conflict by being in the right place, at the right time doing the right thing.Remember, out of sight, out of mind!

Be at peace with the fact that there is only so much you can do

The fact that you are a subordinate means that you have very little influence on your superior's personality traits. There are times when they are critical and others overly-critical. But the good news is that you can still earn their trust and respect. The only downside to that is that you might have to endure too many interactions that are draining. Just do what is right and let the rest be decided by fate!

Seek mentorship and support elsewhere

Now, you have a perfectionist boss who is supposed to be your mentor, but the truth is that they have set unreasonable standards you cannot attain. This means that if you take them as mentors, you will strain yourself too much just to earn their praise.

Perfectionists make very poor mentors!

While we all need support at one point or another, you cannot find it from your perfectionist boss. The truth is that such people tend to hurt your self-image even more. The last thing you want is having your self-worth determined by people who already think that everyone but them is worthy.

Jump ship when you have to

Consider that dealing with such a boss is something that you have to adapt to and not accept it indefinitely. You must know when to cut the cord. The trick is for you to earn their recommendation and move on. This might mean that you seek employment elsewhere.

Start planning your exit strategy as early as you can.

Control Freaks
Let us consider the following situations;

You want to hang out with a friend you met recently, but then your long-term friend insists that you should not because you have not known them well enough to hang out with. This friend asks that if you are going to hang out, you must tell them where exactly you will be meeting when - date and time.

Does this sound familiar?

Well, the truth is that this has happened to us – whether by partners, friends, or family members.

Such kind of people is referred to as control freaks. Dealing with such types of people is not fun – no matter how much they mean to you. It could be that they are doing it because their heart is in the right place, or they mean you no harm, but this is entirely lethal force you don't want to mess with.

You may be thinking, but who exactly is a control freak? Well, a control freak simply refers to perfectionists who feel vulnerable to anything that seems to them as uncontrollable.

The term "control freak" is a psychology-related slang. It describes a person who wants to dictate what everyone does and how everything is done around them. People who have an extremely high need for control over others are considered as control freaks.

Their main attempt is to hide their vulnerabilities by ensuring that everything within their surroundings is under their control. They try hard to manipulate people and put so much pressure on them just so that they don't have to change themselves. Everywhere you go, you will spot a control freak – whether at home, school, or workplace.

With the right strategies up your sleeve, you can deal with them and live a happy life.

Get rid of turf wars

So many control freaks often feel the need to retain control of each aspect of their work just because they do not want to lose their status. It could be that there was a time when they were the only employee in the office and were used to doing all things by themselves. The problem with these kinds of people is the fact that they are very difficult to handle because of their resistance to change – especially growth and expansion.

The real problem is that they feel that the person who has just joined the workplace is out to get "their" job. At first, they did not need any help, and now, they still think that they don't need any help whatsoever. It does not matter how competent the other person is because the control freak will not welcome any ideas or suggestions that are not theirs.

To deal with such a person; what you need to do

is get rid of turf wars by ensuring that you engage them fully during role allocation. Allow them to create their projects so that they feel as though they have a sense of tenure. If it is possible, you can separate their duties from those of other employees. Once they see that their roles are highly valuable to the company, they will ease off on their controlling attitude – giving the others ample space and time to go about their duties with minimal interruptions.

Stroke their ego

According to research, there is evidence that shows control freaks are often very insecure. The thing with such people is that they often fight just so that they can retain control, considering that they are not sure of themselves. Such people hate trying new things and desperately are afraid of new situations and events. They feel that by retaining control over their work surrounding – something familiar to them – they can keep their insecurities in check.

Well, unfortunately, the approach they use in controlling things and people around them depicts their domineering and overbearing attitudes. This is precisely what stands to undermine their self-esteem and confidence further – especially if they spent the time to evaluate their behaviors honestly.

To deal with such kind of people, you need to find a way to help them regain their control so that they can feel secure. The best way to do this is for you to appeal to their ego. While they may come off as confident people, the truth is that inside, they are fragile. They are just hiding under that assertive shell so that they can win others' approval. Before they can offer you any help, go to them and ask them to help you with a difficult task. Even when you feel as though things are not looking up, simply compliment them on anything so that they can relax and make it easier for them to relinquish control over small things.

Stand your ground

There are instances when you feel that there is nothing you can do to appease someone who is controlling. This is because they firmly believe that they know best. They will even go as far as throwing tantrums if they don't get their way.

The best way to handle them is to try and assess what it is that you disagree on. If it is something important, you should stand your ground. While this may stir up conflict and friction at the workplace, it will help them know that not everyone can toy around. The trick is that you choose your battles with caution. If it is an issue of how the office should be cleaned, ask yourself whether it is something you would want to die for.

Take note of the little things

Just like stroking their ego, taking note of small things is about paying attention to what their needs are. Whatever it is, ensure that you pay attention to these tendencies. Reassure them that they are doing an incredible job. Tell them that the place would not be as excellent as it is without them. Praise them for their underlying qualities, and before long, you will realize that their controlling attitude reduces significantly as they soak in praise!

Give a little

Is there someone in your office or home that thinks they know so much more than anyone else? Does it even matter that they believe this? Well, the truth is that in the grand scheme of things, the question that truly matters is if this person is involved in all your daily activities and your ability to do your job. If they don't stand in the way of you getting your job done, the best way to tame them would be to give to her selfish and immature attitude – and simply move on.

Ask questions

One thing you will note about a control freak is that they often are obnoxious. Several people around them dismiss them because of their bossy attitude and desire to control every little thing. Well, the truth is that in reality, they just desire to be part of something – and can offer valuable input – if only people would listen.

Therefore, the next time you encounter a control freak at home or in the office, and they want to boss you around, ask them pointed questions about how they want this or that to be done. If they insist on installing the lights in a specific manner, ask them why they think it cannot be done differently. It could be that they have a phobia for heights, and that is why they insist that it be done a different way than that avoids falling. This allows you to realize that these control issues do not hurt and have the potential of affecting their security in the workplace or at home.

If they are adamant that stationeries go to the right side of their desk and then picture frames on the left, demand for an explanation, there are times when you will realize that they don't have a valid reason for that. If it is not their desk, then that is unacceptable. However, if it is their desk, the best thing is for you to oblige. The point is for you to help them confront their obsessions so that you can know whether there is an actual control issue going on or there is something else subtler that goes beyond stationeries.

Spending time with them talking about these issues will help both of you resolve the problems amicably so that you can both get back to what matters and be productive at it.

If necessary, enlist the help

What if you are not able to reach a point of compromise with someone who is a control freak? In such a case, you can seek advice from your superiors or line manager. You must try to explain to them that your intention is not to cause disharmony in the office. Instead, what you are interested in is creating an atmosphere where each one of you can thrive.

This will also go a long way in helping the boss

understand that you are not there to complain but that you have the company's best interest at heart. You must tell your manager that the other person's tendencies are getting in the way of you working and reaching your goals. Ask them to clarify what your roles and responsibilities are at the office. There is a chance that the management has no idea of what the situation is like, and asking them to step in will help a great deal to clear things up.

It is also essential that you are always ready to offer possible solutions to the issue so that your bosses are aware that you are also a team player. While working with someone who is controlling can be difficult, realize that it does not have to be impossible! Just a little effort aimed at understanding their motivations and alleviating their insecurities will go a long way in helping you work together in harmony.

Narcissists

Narcissists are people who are ready challenging to work mainly because of their big ego and vanity. The problem with them is that they pretend to know it all. If you have such a person at home or the workplace, you must determine where they are real experts and where they are pretentious.

If they are real experts, then your research should prove that they are knowledgeable in that area because of the validity of their ideas and information. You must not subjugate their ideas or permit any condescension. The trick is for you to be respectful when dealing with them. Where you feel they are wrong, simply correct them without being confrontational or overly aggressive.

Gossips
With the advent of technological devices, gossiping is no longer restricted to the water cooler. Today, people gossip with ease of emails and social media platforms. What is interesting is that in spite of all these technological innovations, chatting today at the office or home can be traced back to one single individual who

always knows and shares information – whether true or false.

If you have such a person in your life, the best way to deal with them is to avoid sharing information with them or someone close to them. You must practice remaining cordial when around them. Whenever they try to pry into your life or that of others, gently pull away from the conversation and change the subject into something more productive and useful.

Bullies

These people are a fact of life, and the most unfortunate thing is that by the time they are graduating high school, if they will not have changed, then chances are that they will never change. These are the kind of people who end up taking their insecurities to the workplace, marriages, and friendships. The problem is thinking of others as weak and susceptible and hence use that to be vindictive. They will always try to get other people to gang up against one or more people around them.

When you are dealing with such a person, you must try as much as you can to hide your weaknesses. Stand up to them, and don't tolerate them being respectful to you. Don't get me wrong; I don't mean that you get aggressive with them. However, you must not allow them to interfere with your life. If they try to bring their attitude to your place of work or home, simply ask them to leave.

Slackers

These are the kind of people who are not motivated and are unreliable. They are the kind that cannot carry their weight. If you have never worked with one of these, thank you, God! They are the kind of people who will leave all the work to you. When you are asked to partner with them, ensure that the job assigned to them is done to completion. If not, then you should be prepared to take on their portion of work.

Trust me; they are out there to let people down – beware!

Pessimists

Some people view the world through shades of gray. They are the pessimists whose primary agenda is to dismiss every idea someone comes up with without necessarily offering an alternative. Much of their time is spent complaining about this or that. If you have such a person in your team, the trick is to remain positive. Remind them that you cannot just sit and do nothing; instead, they should give their contributions as well.

Oh, and be prepared to shoulder much of the work!

The hostile or bossy
The one thing I have learned when dealing with these kinds of people is that strength and tact goes a long way. People who feel as though they have been wronged tend to be violent.

The other trick is for you to try as much as you can to help them meet their needs without necessarily being aggressive or discriminatory about it. Try to stay away from any interaction with them that stirs up intense emotions like violence – as they say, don't hang out with the enemy when they are carrying a weapon or drinking! Check your actions to ensure that they don't stir up anger. In short, try not to be a pushover.

The worst thing you can do is strongly retaliate against an aggressive person. Remember that hostility often begets hostility. The best thing you can do is try to divert their attention to something more meaningful. This way, their anger tends to go down. Try to explain to them more about the situation pointing out common interests so that they are open to calm and rational ways of resolving the issue at hand.

The chronic complainer
These are the kind of people who will always find fault in everything you do. They will go to the extent of blaming you. They pretend as though they know all that should be done when, in fact,

they are never open to correcting the situation themselves in the first place.

If you want to cope with these kinds of people, the first thing is for you to pay attention to all they have to say and then ask questions to seek clarification – even though you have been falsely accused or are guilty. The secret is for you not to complain, apologize, or be overly-defensive. If you do, then you are causing them to restate their concerns in a more heated manner. You must be severe and supportive of it. Accept the facts and get all the complaints in writing. Involve them in the process so that you all actively find the solution. Rather than dwelling too much on what is wrong, try to get them to think of what should be done.

The Super-Agreeable

Has anyone ever agreed with everything and anything you say to the point that they make you angry? Well, these are the super-agreeable people. While it is a good thing to get along with people at home and the workplace, some people agree with every idea you give, and then when things suddenly go south; they back down.

What you need to note about these people is that they are after approval. We all come from different family backgrounds with diverse upbringings. Some learned that the best way to get love is through pretense. In the same way, those people who are super-agreeable tend to promise heaven on earth but cannot deliver that. They will tell you, "I will submit the report tomorrow, or I will help you run errands." Don't be fooled; all they are doing is buttering you up.

The best way to handle them is to assure them that it is okay to say "No" when they feel like they will not be able to deliver. It is okay to speak the truth even when it is hard to spit it out. You must take time to ask them to try and be candid so that they can find it easy to come out and be frank about anything. When you support them overcome this habit, they will stop making promises they know they couldn't possibly keep.

Show them that you value the relationship you have, and the truth won't hurt. Ensure that you let them know you are ready to compromise, considering that they will be fair and just.

Critics

"It's hard to kiss the lips at night that chew your butt all day long."

- Former Congressman Ed Foreman

Criticism is not all that bad, but the truth is that there are times and places for it. Debates are where the most effective solutions are birth. This is where some of the best minds challenge every point of view in the room.

But is that always the case with criticism? Are there demanding critics?

Indeed, there are so many demanding critics whose criticism is destructive. They are not seeking answers. They are not even concerned with the give and take that leads to a strong team and a consensus. They are the people who behave like politicians. I like to think of critics as spectators and not players.

Look around your office; is there is a critic there? Is your spouse or friend a critic?

Often, you will notice that critics are the kind of people who will always be quick to point a finger, and yet when their help is needed, they will not lift one. They are the kind of people who will not cooperate within the project, and it is their negative attitude that makes it hard to work and achieve the set goals in a team.

Liars
"Honesty pays, but it doesn't seem to pay enough for most people."

- Kim Hubbard

This saying is sad, but it is probably right. Think about it, if you have a project you are working on, and the members of your team don't want to cooperate and are dishonest, will the project mandate be fulfilled?

The chances are that you will not even have a team to work in the first place. Honesty goes a long way in fostering cooperation, teamwork, and productive working relationships. If you lack trust, then you can't work together peacefully. You cannot be productive.

If you think about lies, the truth is that they come in so many different forms. It could be that little white lie you tell a client to impress them or those you say your spouse so that they are not upset. They could be the lies you show potential employers when you are trying to get them to hire you. One recruiter once said, the closest anyone comes to perfection is when they are trying to fill out a job application. There are three kinds of lies, according to the former Prime Minister of Great Britain; statistics, lies, and darned lies.

Whatever kind of lies you tell; the truth is that it is difficult to deal with a liar. The thing with lying is that it is rarely necessary. It does not matter how distasteful the truth is, the truth is more comfortable to accept than a lie. Once you tell one lie, it spirals and continues for as long as you take it. By the time you realize it, you have caused so much harm than good. The thing with liars is that they will always tell a lie to cover up the first lie.

If there is someone that is always lying, simply talk to them about the value of the truth. Don't try to look down on them. Help them always tell the truth by holding them accountable for their word – bitter or sweet.

Chapter 3 Common traits of difficult people

Everything is about them

Have you ever noticed that there are people who are masters at spinning things – conversations and situations – so that it is about them? Such people often have a way of doing all it takes to bring the discussion back to them when they realize that it has veered off, and the spotlight is no longer on them.

The truth is, interacting with such people is boring. The reason is that whenever you start discussions with them, you are almost sure that the story will be tied to them – how they spent the weekend, what their thoughts are, what ideas they have, or everything else going on in their lives.

Many people ask themselves why they even do it in the first place. Well, the truth is that difficult people are not necessarily cruel. The thing is that they are experiencing a slight immaturity in their personal growth.

They are so used to unabashed attention such that everything is about them and have no time to think of what others think or have to offer too. In worst-case scenarios, everyone that is around them is only there to boost their ego and make them the center of the universe.

They are verbally toxic

Difficult people always have something nasty to say about almost everything. If they are not gossiping, then they are blaming or whining or busy shouldering off responsibilities to the next person they want to bully or use.

In short, these people don't even know when the right time to shut up is. They will always run their mouths about this or that – a typical master storyteller. If someone at home or the workplace experience something even in private, they want to be the first ones to break the news to the whole world – especially those who might be interested.

However, if the news does not seem so unusual, they choose to stand on it on their own two feet. What is worst is that they try to add in salt and sugar just so that the story is compelling – talk of fiction!

Just like the first trait, this reason why they choose to do this is so that they can be the center of attention. What is funny is that instead of making the whole story about them, they choose to be the traveling poet who is busy distributing the news everywhere. They do this so that they can control everything that people know.

They paint themselves as victims

The other trait you will notice with difficult people is that you cannot tell them anything because they tend to portray themselves as less-than-charming. For instance, if you call them out on something, they will suddenly become emotional and start apologizing profusely. As they do this, they give people a million and one reasons for their actions.

It could be that they are behaving in this manner because they were not brought up in a loving family, or that they are insecure about something from their childhood. It could also be that they have an incredibly rare mental disorder that causes them to act this way.

Their behavior is a prime example of what deflection is all about. While there are some of these people who are consciously unaware of what they are doing, there are instances where some have adopted this kind of defense mechanism from their childhood into adulthood, and everything seems reasonable to them.

Often oblivious to the obvious

Whenever you meet someone trying, one thing you need to bear in mind is that you are not the only one that feels that way. Someone difficult to you will always be trying to everyone around them.

The lives of difficult people are filled with several people interested in confronting their challenging behavior. You will find their families sighing about it, people looking at them with sneering at them by the roads, or coworkers having disgruntled faces whenever they meet by the corridors. However, no matter what happens, these signs don't seem enough for them.

They choose to be oblivious about it all so that they can keep behaving in the same way.

The main reason why they do this is that they have an abundance of pride or are simply not aware of their behavior.

They count everything
The thing with difficult people is that they will never do anything and be quiet about it. They have to go on and on about what they have done. Whenever they are asked to do anything that goes beyond their usual roles and responsibilities, they will ensure that you pay them for it. Even once you have paid them, they will remind you over and over again that they did you a favor and will use that to get what they want.

The main reason is that they are too self-absorbed – something that causes them to be too self-serving. Each minute they use doing a task that is not directly linked to their interests; they will live in anguish.

That said, a difficult person is one that will never exemplify all the typical traits we have discussed in this chapter. Instead, they often tend to have a different blend of problematic characteristics that cause them to be complicated.

We all certainly have at least one or two of these traits that make as demanding in one way or the other. By recognizing these features, we can act on them, work on fixing them – whether in us on the people around us – so that we can all live a happy and free life.

Chapter 4

Identifying the complicated issue

What will get you ready and self-aware whenever tough situations involving difficult people arise is if you choose to turn the situation inward and analyze each trigger and reaction. According to Elizabeth B. Brown, there is a wide range of questions you need to reflect on for you to better understand the root cause of issues and why the other person involved is driving you crazy. These questions include;

- What are the emotional tornadoes that the problematic person brings to your life?
- **What is your reaction to the difficult person?**
- How do they respond to your reactions?
- **If the other person in your life is the cause of all problems, have you found ways to grow unhealthy**

actions and responses towards them?

- Is it possible that you are a difficult person driving others crazy?

- **If that is the case, how do they choose to respond to your actions and responses?**

When you are trying to deal with a difficult person, the last thing you want is to feed into your frustrations. The truth is that when you do this, you are just continuing a vicious cycle that will not end. The problem with most people is that they tend to see or to hear things the way they want to and then interpret them based on assumptions rather than facts and actions.

Unfortunately, we often lack information on why one shows up the way they are. This explains the reason why often, we fill in the blanks with our theories and assumptions because we don't have the facts or do not want to find them in the first place.

Mitigating These Situations

If you are going to deal with the difficult people in your life objectively, you have to be willing to separate facts from assumptions or theories. It is often beneficial to try and separate ourselves from our negative emotional feelings that we may be experiencing at that very moment. While this may be easier said than done, those who can get to this point can arm themselves with the power of friendly and productive interactions with people who make them cringe.

To achieve this, you must use the three different lenses to have a general outlook of the world. These lenses include;

Realistic optimism lens

To use this lens, you must start by asking yourself two simple questions whenever you feel that someone has unfairly treated you. These questions include;

What is the factual information in this case?

Is there a story I am telling myself about these facts? What is it that I anticipate as an outcome?

The reverse lens

This kind of glass requires that you look at the world around you through a glass of the person that triggered you. Well, don't get me wrong – I don't mean that you should sacrifice your own opinion just so that you can make others happy. Instead, you must widen your perspective. Using the reverse lens, you need to ask yourself;

- What is the other person feeling? How do their feelings make sense?
- What is my responsibility in all these?

You may see this as counterintuitive at first, but the truth is that this is something compelling in helping you reclaim your value. Whenever you feel threatened, you must find a way to appreciate yourself and the other person, too – this is essentially what we refer to as empathy.

The long lens

Did you know that at times the worst fears you have about the other person may turn out to be true? Most difficult people I know often derive satisfaction from unreasonably bullying others. If you choose to see things from their perspective, that might not make sense at all. These are the people that will take credit for your work. When and if this happens to you, the first question you need to ask yourself is, "irrespective of what I feel at this moment, is there a way I can learn and grow from this experience?"

Realize that when you are dealing with difficult people – irrespective of what their personality traits are – there are essential steps that you must take to make the best of the whole situation. You can work hard towards finding a more productive outcome. We will discuss this in detail in the next chapter.

How to manage your reactions

Managing your reactions and emotional feelings are all about taking in deep breathes. According to research, slow and deep breaths go a long way in triggering something below the spine – referred to as the Vagus nerve – which transmits neurotransmitters to the brain to calm down.

You must ensure that you take a moment to reflect on how you are feeling. The most important thing is for you to ask yourself how you would like to respond to those emotional feelings. Is it possible for you to create a good outcome from the situation?

Well, this may feel at first as though it is an overkill. However, realize that this will get your brain out of its automatic response. You will not feel that negativity, sharpness, and defensiveness anymore. When you force yourself to think of ways that create positive outcomes, your brain automatically assumes a positive mode of thinking.

Leveraging self-control

If you are going to handle every difficult situ with a difficult person in an amicable manner, you must know yourself. When you have a clear sense of who you indeed are, what it is that stirs up the tension, and where your limits are, you will be better off socializing with people however difficult they may prove to be. You must learn how to stay calm, develop your awareness and skills in emotional intelligence so that you can effectively manage your reactions to every frustrating situation.

Today, challenge yourself to always start by seeking to understand the situation at hand better. When you have more clarity about the situation – by asking questions – you will not only manage your reactions better but also help you find a mutually satisfactory outcome. Reflect on what it is that you consider a satisfactory result before you can interact with difficult people so that you better place to keep your focus on what truly matters in the first place.

The other trick is for you to ensure that you stick to the facts and acknowledge your emotions. When you make use of examples rather than interpretations, you will be able to keep your interactions with difficult people in check. Before you can respond to what it is that they said, ensure that you paraphrase and check the accuracy of their words so that you have a good understanding of what they mean rather than choosing to make assumptions by hearing what you want to hear. When you check for the accuracy of the information first before responding, this is an indicator that you want to work with others effectively.

When you respond by stating your emotions or what impact their words have on you, this can be a great nudge that will help the other person realize that what they are doing is wrong and hurtful. If there is something you think is not right, it is better if you seek the help of others.

The truth is that you are not alone in this.

Some so many other people have been through what you are experiencing at the moment. Their experiences may have been productive when dealing, working, or interacting with someone difficult. When you seek their advice or coaching from someone experienced, this can go a long way in helping you overcome. Research shows that when you talk about your feelings, you will be in a better position to reframe the whole situation to a place where you can effectively facilitate a positive result.

Where necessary, ensure that you keep records. There are times when things get a little bit more abrasive to the point where you run the risk of hitting an end-state you never intended in the first place. If the interaction gets to the point where it is toxic, you must start making intentional efforts to document them. This means that when things begin to go south, you will have an excellent map to lead you to a place of restoration and peace.

Chapter 5

Developing Coping and Negotiation strategies

As you may already have learned, difficult people are everywhere. There is a chance that you, too, are difficult. The truth is that several people struggle to go through periods where they are not in their best behaviors. If you desire to maintain a healthy working relationship with someone difficult, then it is high time you learned some of the most practical and helpful coping and negotiation strategies that will make your life easy.

Here are some;

Method 1 Approach the problematic person
Step 1 Choose your battles carefully
When you are butting heads with someone

difficult, the most important thing for you is to decide when you think your efforts will yield fruit – that is when you go ahead to discuss the issue at hand. Realize that not every fight that comes your way is worth fighting. The sooner you realize that battles are to be chosen wisely, the better you will be.

In an ideal world, both you and the difficult person would simply set your differences aside and make compromises. While this is often impossible, what you need to ask yourself in such a situation is whether the issue is so distressing that you must address it right there and then. Consider your relationship with this person. If you are at loggerheads with your boss or someone in authority, then the sooner you accept the things you cannot change, the happier you will be. If the issue arises between you and a member of your family, then you have to choose between saving your time, efforts, and grief, or whether enabling a bad behavior is a preference.

Take a step back and think whether by fighting the battle, you stand to win. You can only take on someone that irks you once you have assessed the whole situation and consider whether there is a possible resolution to it. If the timing is not right, then take time to formulate a plan, seek help, wait for the right time or find another practical option.

Step 2 Take a pause

Before you respond to any situation, the first thing is for you to take in a deep breath. This will allow you to recollect all your thoughts, calm your mind, and your emotional feelings. If you are dealing with a problematic person via a mobile text message or email or other digital means, try as much as you can not to send anything that might stir up the war further. Allow your stress levels to come down first before you can approach the other person and reason together.

Try also to have a neutral meeting place where you both can discuss the issue. For instance, you could talk over the issue while taking a walk or doing something else. The importance of this is to try and limit one-on-one negative interaction.

Step 3 Clearly state your needs with assertive communications

The thing with difficult people is that when you try to communicate with them and have a reasonable discussion, they will try to manipulate you or twist your words around. The best way you can avoid that is by using the 'I' statement instead of 'you' that may sound accusative.

Let us consider an instance where someone has been consistently late to work the whole week. Now, if their boss is the difficult one, simply say, "I understand that you are mad at me for being late this week. That is precisely how I would feel. Unfortunately, our subway line is under construction, hence the constant delays at the station. My apologies for making you wait every morning this week. "

This is different from saying something like: "You

are such an unreasonable person for expecting me to get to work on time when the subway is under construction. You don't care about anything but your work. If you did, you could have already paid attention to the news and known that the line had issues."

The first response is the best one. It shows your remorse for being late, your respect for the boss, and your plan to resume routine once the subway has been completed. You must try as much as possible to sandwich your response while talking to someone difficult. Always start with a positive comment to show how much you value the relationship between the two of you. Then head right into the tough part of the conversation. Finally, complete it with a positive remark like thanking them for lending you a listening ear.

Step 4 Keep being polite

My grandmother always said that being polite is something that will not cost you anything but will earn you every good thing. The same applies when dealing with someone difficult. It does not matter what the difficult person's response is because what truly counts is how you respond to it. If you keep your cool, things will always not escalate out of control.

Several people get in the trap of name-calling and abusive behaviors. The trick is for you to take a step back, take in a deep breath, and then give your response politely. Try as much as you can not allow yourself to sink into the other person's level. The calmer you remain, the higher the likelihood of the other person noticing and trying to mirror your behavior.

It all starts with how you respond!

Ensure that you do it right.

Step 5 Stick to the facts

Have you ever tried arguing with someone whose speech is all over the place – throws around claims and accusations – without really taking the time to substantiate their claims? This can be annoying!

When dealing with a difficult person, the trick is to keep your conversation short, clear, and to the point. It does not add any value bogging it all down with too many unnecessary details that will only stir up negative emotions. The chances are that you will not successfully get to them enough for them to see your point of view. There is no need to convince them. Simply state what took place, and don't try to explain yourself.

You must avoid all forms of triggers. If you always fight about holidays with your brothers, stay away from the whole topic. Instead, allow someone neutral to mediate. Don't try to be defensive. Yes, you might want to argue your point, but if it is with a difficult person, you had better skip the whole argument. It does not add any value trying to prove you are right. Let the situation stay as neutral as you possibly can.

Step 6 Minimize your interactions
It is one thing to be hopeful about dealing with

the issues you have with the difficult person and get the desired outcome. However, the best advice you can give yourself is to try and avoid spending too much time with them. If you must interact, then keep it short. You can excuse yourself from all conversations or even bring on a third-party. Throughout the interview, ensure that you stay positive and always try to calm down afterward. Just accept that this problematic person might never be the colleague, neighbor, friend, or sibling you ever wanted to have – and that is okay.

Step 7 Talk to allies

If you are not getting along with someone and you think that you should, then it helps to find a potential mediator to help bring the two of you together. If you are colleagues, then perhaps your boss can help make the situation better. If the conflict is within your family, then you can reach out to a mutual neutral party to help you negotiate. The point is for you always to seek to share complaints with those you trust only.

Method 2 Change your mindset
Step 1 Realize that there will always be difficult people anyway

As we have already mentioned, you will ever encounter difficult people everywhere you go. There will always be people out there who are looking for someone to hurt. The key here is for you to learn how you can deal with such people. While they may be impossible to avoid, you must take time to study their personality traits so that you better place to deal with them.

For instance, if the person is a hostile type, you may notice that they are cynical, think that they are always right, and are argumentative. These are mostly people who do well in authority or power roles. If it is someone that is emotionally sensitive, they will always look for insults – are easily offended, hence choose to use textual approaches when expressing their disappointments and anger. Egotists, on the other hand, are concerned with their selfish interests without really caring much about what

84

others want – often loathe compromise, ungrateful and insensitive. Finally, Neurotic types are those who are anxious, overly critical, and pessimistic.

Step 2 Increase of frustration tolerance

You can control a bird from building a nest on your head, but you cannot prevent them from crossing over your head. In other words, the other person's behavior is something that is beyond your control, but your reaction to them is within your control. You are the one to choose whether or not to engage them. To achieve this, you must be ready to build your frustration tolerance – which involves you taking the lead at challenging irrational beliefs that might contribute to stress, anger, and outbursts.

When you are interacting with a difficult person, you may think that you are unable to deal with them. Those are just irrational thoughts trying to scare you off. The best approach is for you to take in a deep breath and then question the validity of that thought.

In reality, you can deal with anything you put your mind to. If your mother-in-law is trying to micromanage you in your own house, you will not go crazy because you can deal with that. You are stronger than you give yourself credit. The trick is for you to fine-tune your mind to handle it. Instead of stressing over it and causing yourself harm, take in a deep breath and hand her some work to do so that she is occupied. Watch the words you use and ensure that they are rational.

Step 3 Examine your behavior

If you find that people continuously attack you, then the chances are that you are attracting the wrong crowd. If you are overly negative, the chances are that you will attract a group of pessimistic people who will flock around you.

To deal with fire, you have to arm yourself with fire. To attract positivity, you have to engage in positive behaviors. Think back to all the negative experiences that you might have gone through and ask yourself what your role was in them.

How did you respond to the other person's behavior? At the office, there may be someone that always picks on you – how you talk, dress, work, or do things at work – how do you respond to them? Do you have the power to stand up for yourself? Take time to recognize all your strengths and weaknesses so that you are better placed to confront the difficult person in a way that puts them in their place.

Step 4 Beware of your perceptions of others

Have you ever thought that maybe the reason why your friend is acting up is that they are going through a rough patch in their lives? While that is no excuse for their behavior, you must not be quick to judge others behavior. Take time to practice empathy. Simply take a step behind and reflect on how you would respond if you were in a similar situation. Your sensitivity to differences in personality might just be the reason why you hand a wide range of conflicts.

The trick is for you to learn how to practice

acceptance. Take in a deep breath and look at them with such compassion. Talk to them with so much calm and tell them that you see that they are suffering and in pain. Let them know that you accept the fact that they are scared and anxious, even if you don't understand the reason behind their situation. Let them also know that their situation is making you anxious.

The truth is, when you accept the situation just the way it is, you let go of so much tension that might have stirred up resistance and conflict between the two of you. Yes, you may not understand why your client blew up at you as they did. Rather than becoming angry and snapping back at them, consider the possibility that they may be hurting inside. Whether the reason is valid or not, it will help you stay calm and not yield into the power of negativity.

Chapter 6

Steps on how to deal with a difficult person

If you ask any manager or coach, they will tell you that there is always that one employee that is not so great to work with. As it turns out, management is still there to ensure that within the company's landscape, they are there to oversee the performance of all other employees within their department. This does not mean that being a manager or parent or in a leadership position means that you are not a difficult person to work with. Even those in authority can prove very difficult to deal with, whether at the workplace or home.

The last thing you want is to be held hostage, spend lots of time and emotional energy thinking of how you are going to get your work done without someone standing in the way or trying to make your life a living hell. There are times when you are left debating whether or not to let them go, but you never get around to pulling the trigger.

So, if you are this kind of person that has been pulled by difficult people into the endless vortex of frustration and ineffectiveness, these are the steps you can deal with them gracefully;

Step 1: Listen

Often, when someone is difficult, the truth is that we stop paying attention to what it is that is going on. We get irritated and lose hope in them. We decide what we think of them just so that our focus shifts to something else – because we want to avoid them and protect ourselves from them.

However, if you want to be effective at dealing with them, then you have to be very attentive when they are not doing well or are being hard headed. Your best shot at making things better is seeking to have a clear understanding of the issue – including knowing the other person's viewpoint. In most cases, the first thing that you need to do is simply listen. Listening alone can save the day.

When you listen, you set yourself up to hear what the real problem is, and you may even note that it is not the other person's fault. The truth is that the problematic person might just start acting differently once they know that their concerns have been heard. Not everyone difficult becomes that way just for fun – it could be that there are real issues they are airing, and they need them to be addressed.

Step 2: Offer clear behavioral feedback
If you look around you, you will notice that most people spend weeks, months, or even years complaining about someone in their lives, which is trying. What they don't do is give actual feedback on what it is that they need to change or do differently. You cannot keep doing the same things over and over again, expecting a change each time.

While giving harsh feedback is something that can be uncomfortable for many people, you can choose to do it responsibly. When you change your ways, you will realize that the other person will also change. The approach that you can use to give transparent and honest feedback is first to lower the other person's defensiveness so that you can offer them with the information they need to be better. Whatever approach you choose to use, they must do these two things – and you will be on the right track.

But why do we hate giving feedback, and how can we make it easier?

Well, over the past three decades, my friends and I have worked to train and coach thousands of people to become better managers and leaders, whether at home or in the office. When we asked them what they consider is the toughest part of their daily job, they said giving others corrective feedback – almost without exception.

So many of them said that at work, they find it

hard to fire someone – painful or not. But then this is something that they still have to do, however hard it may be. However, this is not to say that everyone is afraid of giving feedback. There are a handful of other people I know who are not afraid to give people harsh feedback.

But really, the question is, why is it hard for you to give your employees, friends, or spouse difficult feedback to tell them that they are doing something wrong and they need to change?

Well, the truth is that we are often afraid of how these people will react. We think to ourselves, they are already complicated, what if they explode in anger? What if they break down? What if they respond by telling me that I am an idiot? What if they become defensive and start blaming me. There are times when we want to tell someone that their attitude is terrible, but we stop and think of what it is that they might say; "you don't even have respect for me. You don't care about what I am going through," - all of which worsen the situation.

With all these myriads of thoughts racing through our minds, we convince ourselves that it is not a big deal at all. We tell ourselves that it will all go away soon. We tell ourselves that if they are the right person, they will realize that what they are doing is wrong, and they will just let it all go away. While this will make you feel justified and self-righteous, the truth is that you are causing more harm than good. There are people I have seen lose their jobs just because their bosses or the people in their lives chickened out and did not tell them what they are doing is not alright. They needed your corrective feedback, but you did not give them. Some people cannot magically know that they are difficult and that they need to change. They need you to be their eyes!

Here are the tips you can use;

Pay attention first
While this might seem counterintuitive at first when you know that you have screwed your

courage, you just need to stand up and get it over with. The first thing is for you to listen to what the other person has to say. Walk up to them and tell them that you would like to talk to them about something. Invite them to share with you what their view is about the whole situation.

For instance, you could say something like, "Hey Mary, I'd like to have a word with you about the ABC project. What time are you available for a chat?" Once you meet, you can ask them, "what do you think has been working well, and what has not been working well on the ABC project?"

When you do this, you are merely offering the other person a heads-up on what you would like to discuss. You are telling them that you would love to have a balanced picture of the whole project – not just focusing on the good news but the bad news as well.

Then give them ample time to share with you their opinion. Try not to interrupt – whether in agreement or disagreement - when they are talking to you. This way, you will be able to gather what it is that the other person thinks so that you have all the information you need to give a more objective response. You may realize that the other person will say so much of what you were going to say too. This way, the conversation turns into a coaching session!

Often, you will notice that the other person will see part of the problem and that allows you to pick it up from there and clarify what they have said. Now, if the other person is entirely oblivious to the whole situation, listening first to what they have to say makes the entire conversation less adversarial. This allows them to listen to you better when you start giving them your take on the issue.

Camera check

The other useful tip you must consider is what I refer to as the camera check. This is mainly feedback on people's behaviors rather than on their mental state. Let us go back to the example that we have already used in the previous point where you think that the employee has a bad attitude.

Now, at this point, you know that if you just say it plainly, that will not help, and the chances are that it will make the situation worse than it is. Such a comment is guaranteed to make the other person feel defensive because it mentions that they have a flawed character. You also are giving the other person no indication of what it is that you want them to do differently, which they don't have an idea how. How does the right attitude look like?

Rather than jumping in and making these comments without basis, simply do a camera check. In other words, what you need to do is take a mental video of what you consider a bad attitude and the other person doing it. What is it that you see in your mental tape? You might see them coming to work late, turning in their assignments late, saying negative things about their colleagues or the company, consistently not offering support to clients, among others.

These are some of the things that you can tell them. "Hey Mary, I notice that you have been turning in your assignments late, coming to work late this month, and saying negative things about your colleagues – Mark and Jane." When you frame it this way, you make it a hell LOT more comfortable for the other person to hear, rather than just saying that they have a bad attitude.

The point is, if someone is difficult, you can camera check what you consider to be an evil character or attitude and frame it in that manner. This is reasonably comfortable and skillful when trying to offer corrective feedback. When you let them know what it is they need to do differently for improvement and success, you are not only helping them be better but also yourself and the organization as a whole.

Step 3: Document

I can't stress this enough, but whenever you have significant issues with someone, you must jot down all the key points. There are several times when I have had people in top management levels tell me that they couldn't let go of a difficult employee because they did not have a record of them having bad behavior. It is this lack of documentation that comes as a result of misplaced hopelessness. The manager either thought that they did not want to be too negative about the employee or believed that it would soon go away.

If you are smart enough, then you know the value of documentation. You are keeping a record of each employee or person in your life, and what good and evil they do is nothing negative. If anything, it is something very prudent. What you need to note is that you can solve problems. All you need to do is take in a deep breath, follow it with a sigh of relief and write down everything you like or do not like about the other person –

everything they are doing that qualifies as bad or good behavior.

You will thank yourself for it when "enough is enough!"

Step 4: Maintain consistency

If there is a behavior that you consider not okay with, then there should not be a time when you all of a sudden are okay with it. Remember that where you are, people are watching you. The last thing you want has everyone thinking that you are inconsistent or mistreating others. If it is at the employee, what you must remember is that employees are always looking to see what it is that you do more than you say.

For instance, if you tell everyone that they must turn in their end month reports by Friday Midnight and then there are times when you are upset about it, and in other times you are not, the truth is that they will not take you seriously. Those employees that are difficult won't do it at all.

You must learn to pick your shots. Set standards that you are willing to hold to – then hold tightly to them.

Step 5: Establish consequences for when things don't change

If, at this point, you still feel that there is no improvement, then it is high time you start getting specific. There is a saying, "I believe you can still turn this around," and this is where you apply that. Turning things around simply means that if you don't see behavioral change by a specific date, then something will happen – letting them go, initiate corrective actions, disciplinary committee discussion, or lose their eligibility for promotion.

The consequences have to be substantively negative for them to see the seriousness of the whole issue. If difficult people don't believe that their actions have serious consequences, then what makes you think that they will even change in the first place?

Step 6: Work through the company's processes

What you need to note is that when you are a good manager or leader, you will hold out hope for improvement to the point where you can't see any more hope and decide that you are letting go. You ensure that you have dotted all the I's and crossed every T so that you have a clear conscience when you finally make go of the other person. Maybe this is the point where you are in your marriage, parenting, or at work. If this is the case, then what I would advise you to do is to have a clear conversation with your spouse, boss, or child on what exactly you need to do to clear the whole path to termination – if necessary.

Step 7: Don't poison the well

If there is something I have learned over the years I have worked for my company is the value of not poisoning the well. There are times when junior and senior managers alike come to the office and lousy mouth a problematic employee in their department to all and sundry. This is not the right way to address an issue like this.

Instead, you must follow all the steps that we have highlighted here.

It does not matter how difficult the person is, how crazy they drive you, or how hurtful their actions are. What matters the most is that you don't talk trash about them – you will only be adding salt to injury. Remember that the people you are telling are the same people that will go out there is talk – with distorted information. This will only create an environment of distrust. You will be choosing to back-stab them, something that pollutes the other person's perception. You will also be opening yourself up for the rest of the people to look at you as weak and unprofessional.

Trust me; this is no way to resolve an issue.

Just don't do it – however tempting it may be!

Step 8: Manage your self-talk

There are instances when someone frustrates you to the point where you end up having an inner conversation about the whole issue. While the internal dialogue is calming, it never should be unhelpfully negative or unhelpfully positive.

You may think to yourself, "what an idiot, Mary will never change" or "I will not worry too much about this. I am certain that things will turn out to be fine. Mary is such a great employee or wife or child, and there is nothing to worry about." These two thoughts are not helpful at all.

You must be willing to take a fair witness stance so that everything you say to yourself on the inside is not only accurate but also possible. You could say something like, "Mary's behavior is stirring up problems for the entire family. As I do everything I can to support them to change, I have to monitor their behavior closely. If the change, that will be great. If not, then I will have to do what I promised to do."

Now, that is helpful because you are taking the facts and using them to make informed decisions that are not only going to make you look good but are aimed at helping the other individual.

Step 9: Have the courage

By this time, you know that firing someone is the hardest decision most managers have to make. If the difficult person you are dealing with is your spouse, then you know that the toughest decision you are going to make is to seek marriage counseling or divorce. Whatever your situation may be like, the most important thing is that you do it right.

Instead of making excuses, putting things off, or making someone else do it, just brace yourself, gather your courage, and do it yourself. Realize that you are the manager of your life, and if you are as good as you think you are, then you are going to make the tough decision impeccably well. If – Hallelujah – things change against what you hoped for, dare to accept them. Realize that sometimes being proved wrong when we have lost hope in someone is as tough as being proved right.

If you learn to use these steps when dealing with a difficult spouse, colleague, employee, or friend, then it does not matter how things turn out because, in the end, you will know that you did the best you could to salvage a tough situation. That alone is enough to reduce your stress levels!

Chapter 7

What do you do when all these do not work?

This is one of the questions that so many people ask. There are times when we feel that we have done all there was to be done, and we still cannot see any improvement. While we may be tempted to think that there is nothing more we could do, the truth is that there is always something new we can do. If you have reached this point while dealing with someone challenging in your life, here is a message for you – there is still more you can do!

Here are some of the things you can do;

Be calm

Sometimes, you may be tempted to lose your temper and snap at other people. Well, I will tell you that this is not the best way to handle a difficult person. If you go around snapping at other people, don't you think that you are difficult for other innocent people yourself? What makes you think that you are any different from a difficult person? You are not going to get the other person to collaborate with you if this is the attitude you choose to have.

One thing that is important to note is that you cannot trigger the other person – unless you are silently using it as a strategy – it is best if you keep your cool.

One thing you will note about someone calm is that they often appear as though they are in control – even when that is not the case. Keeping your cool tends to help you stay centered and respectable. If you are always on edge, no one would be willing to reason with you. If you keep your cool, you will start noticing that the other difficult person gets all your attention.

Understand the other person's intentions

I believe that no one chooses to be difficult just for the sake of being tough. While there are times when the other person seems as though they intend to get you, you have to realize that there are always underlying reasons why they are acting up the way they do.

Well, this kind of motivation is not always something apparent. The most important thing is for you to identify what triggered their actions. Is there something that is making them act the way they are doing? Are they willing to cooperate with you? If not, what is stopping them from working with you? Is there something you can do to help them amicably resolve the issue?

Get some perspective

There is a chance that the people around you have experienced exactly what you are going through now. The truth is that while this may be happening to you for the very first time, some can help you see things from a different perspective and offer you a different take on the whole situation.

The challenge is for you to try and seek them out, share with them your experience, and then pay attention to what they have to say to you. The chances are that they will offer you valuable advice amid your conversation, and you will have overcome what seemed impossible at first.

Let them know where you are coming from

If anything has worked perfectly for me, it is letting the other person know what my intentions are. I always come clear on why I am doing what I do. While there are times when my words face resistance for thinking that is just being tough on them, the truth is that it works. When you let other people in on the reason underlying your actions and what is happening on the ground, they will not only empathize with the situation but will also change their behaviors. This is how you can get difficult people on board!

Do it today.

Establish a rapport

Today, the use of a computer system in messaging and communication has simply turned work into a mechanical process. The best way you can re-instill that human touch when interacting with others is always set aside time to connect with them at a personal level. You can choose to go out with your friends, family, or colleagues for drinks, lunches, or dinners. When you do, don't just concentrate on what you are eating or drinking, always spend time knowing each other – hobbies, families, life in general. Fostering a valuable connection with others goes a long way in helping you appreciate the beauty in diversity and know how best you can deal with situations that might arise between the two of you.

So, how do you establish rapport?

One important thing that you must note is that building rapport is not just about mirroring, matching, or leading the other person's behavior and actions. When dealing with a difficult person, think of it as a therapy session or sales. If you want your relationship to be productive, then you want to pay attention to the building blocks of good rapport. The general idea here is for you to mirror their posture – such that if they cross their arms while talking to you, you do the same shortly after. You can also speak in the same tone, pace, and language they speak in – adding in a couple of unique phrases and words they use while communicating with you.

When the other person starts to notice these similarities in their unconscious mind, the truth is that they will begin to feel that they are on the same level as you are, like you, and tune in to what you have to say. Little by little, you will start to lead them towards the direction you want them to go. You will begin to make them feel relaxed. If the rapport you develop is sufficient enough, then you will start noticing on your end that the other person is slowing matching your behavior without even realizing it. They may lean back, integrate your ideas, and echo their enthusiasm in all the skills you are trying to bring to life.

Does it all happen in one go? Not. Just like every other good thing, establishing rapport with a difficult person is something that takes time and effort. You have to be persistent and patient enough to see this through. Remember, you are dealing with someone difficult, which means that they are not just going to all of a sudden take up your ideas and support you. The truth is that you will experience moments of resistance, reluctance, and lack of focus on what you are saying. The sooner you make the other person feel heard and understood, the sooner you will be able to connect and integrate therapeutic interventions.

But how can you do that? How is it possible for you to instantly connect with a difficult person, build rapport with them, and make them get where you are coming from?

The power of utilization

Each time you want to have a connection with someone, you will need to use the principle of utilization to build rapport. One of the most straightforward approaches is for you to discuss your experiences and interests as you talk to them, even though you don't share them.

My friend Lance serves in the military. He told me that their former commando was such a difficult person to deal with. He wanted for them to get along, and he just knew the right way how – going into a trance. He said that hypnotic trance simply takes advantage of the narrow focus of attention and the passing of time. He simply re-evoke part of his military exercise to his commando and boom – it was all there in his mind. Now, it made it very easy to lead him one step at a time to where he desired to go – leveraging that alert and focused state of mind. This way, the commando started becoming receptive – by integrating his perspective, ideas, and ability to control pain. By the end of the session, they both were getting along like never before.

Effective communication through the utilization

The other trick is for you to utilize the other person's interests when talking to them. This is one of the most straightforward and powerful tools you can use to capture their attention and get them interested in what you have to say. Once you have them hooked, you can then bring up topics that you find interesting – but do it gradually just so that they don't feel overwhelmed and lose interest. While flirting is something that is not recommended in professional settings, you can bring on the game instinctively!

Realize that even the stand-up comedians don't always bring their comedy to people that love it but to those who think that they are not funny too. How do they get them hooked? By employing the power of utilization. The thing that seems to get people to laugh at their jokes if recognizing that what they are saying is true, but the chances are that they have never tried to put them in words. They also seem to exaggerate things to an entirely absurd level. Why is that? They can utilize what the target audience already understands.

Even though the examples I share here are from a therapeutic field of hypnosis, the principle of utilization goes a long way in communications as well as teaching. If you become too professional, you might just lose them.

Flirt instinctively!

Stop the psych-jargon

Occasionally, meeting someone for the very first time, I can tell whether they are difficult or not, and the ideology that is ingrained in them. While there are people who speak like they have swallowed a self-improvement book, every word they say is plainly but psych-jargon.

With the principle of utilization, all this goes out of the window. If you are going to have any influence on them, you must learn to see things from their perspective, learn their language, and understanding instead of dragging them into your thinking.

If you talk to any hypnotherapist, they will simply hand you ready-made scripts. This is not what you want to do. You cannot just dish out ways the other person should get along with you as though to tell them you don't have the slightest regard for their uniqueness. When you understand and practice the power of utilization, they will start to feel respected. You cannot just force your interests or ideas on the other person.

Instead of trying to change the other person from the outside, why not try changing them from the inside? This means that every action and the word you use must appeal to their unique personality traits and interests. This way, you offer them a chance to grow through progression quite naturally while at the same time facilitating a deeper level of rapport with them.

Let us consider a smoker who is always prone to outbursts. Where do you channel that anger? Well, you can make them direct that anger towards the cigarettes. In doing so, they don't dismiss the reality of their passion but then helps a long way in constructively managing their anger until they know the best way how. You could also argue that when anger is directed towards something potentially harmful, this is completely helpful.

Utilizing the gaping problem

According to Milton Erickson, you can use the difficult person's issues as a way of helping them make progress in life. He narrates a time when he treated a suicidal patient that was convinced life had no meaning because she believed that she was unattractive and could never find a partner. But what did she think was making her unattractive? A gap between her teeth!

Now, you don't just tell that person that they are attractive and ignore all their worries and concerns. What Erickson did was to utilize the very things she worried about just so that she could change her thinking. The girl squirted water through her supposedly "ugly" gap on her teeth during a break at the office. The young man thought of this as a provocative act and asked her out on a date! That completely changed her thought process.

In the same way, you can utilize the power of gaping problems when dealing with a difficult person, and you will be amazed at how fast they begin to change their minds and perspective.

It works!

Treat the other with respect

Do you like being treated as though you are incompetent, stupid, or incapable? Well, no one does, and neither do you. The thing with treatment is that it is two-way traffic. You have to do unto others exactly how you would like them to do unto you. You cannot possibly expect others to respect you when all the time you interact with them, you are disrespectful.

Today, ask yourself how you love others to treat

you. Then use exactly those requirements when interacting with others. Respect is earned – so earn it!

So, how do you even treat a difficult person with respect, in the first place?

Well, if you want to lay the groundwork for respect, here are some of the things that you need to do;

Stop to see where they are coming from

As we have already established, people do not just choose to be difficult for no reason at all. It is not like this is a default setting – even though there are times when it seems like it when trying to manage and work with them. Think about it, if you have a difficult coworker, do you think that they just found themselves in that job? Someone somewhere must have selected them as a candidate out of all others vying for the same position.

Why is that?

Because they brought onto the job skills and personality that would get things done, if you think about it, they probably fit in well with the rest of the team at the beginning. However, if they no longer embody these traits and skills, the only honest thing to do is stop and find the reason why. Is there something in the job description that has changed? Are they having trouble finding the right balance with their work and private life? Is there someone on the job that keeps irritating them every other day?

When you set aside time to have an honest and open discussion with them concerning all the challenges they may be facing, this could help. While this is a necessary step in addressing the problem, it is something tricky to do. Therefore, rather than getting frustrated, open yourself up for a candid conversation with them.

Trust them first
If you want to build respect with a difficult person, you have to start by building trust. This is

one of the most critical steps, especially in an instance where the other person does not trust you. A difficult person that does not trust you at all with always challenge you at every level. To give the benefit of the doubt, choose to believe them first.

While you may have the authority to manage their actions, the truth is that you cannot change their attitude. It does not matter what position you hold in the company; the truth is that the only way out is to try and influence them. Whenever you make promises, ensure that you live up to them. Do everything that you said you would do – and this will earn you trust. Soon enough, everyone around you will take your word for it and know that you expect nothing less from them. When you trust them to do the same, you are opening doors for higher results and respect.

Pay attention to the positive
As you work hard to establish trust and respect with the difficult person in your life, the one thing

you must not forget is to offer positive feedback. You can do this by way of appreciation. Are there areas that the difficult person is trying hard to improve? If there are, recognize them in front of the whole team. To make it even better, you can take a step further to ask them what it is that they think is the best trait they possess at work and then recognize it too.

In so doing, you are demonstrating to them that they truly matter, and their contributions are much appreciated. You can understand them vocally whenever they do something commendable. Soon enough, they will realize that they are an essential part of the team. To earn your employees respect or anyone for that matter, you have to show them that you value them.

It all starts with you!

Have a new perspective
What is the bottom line of respect? Well, the truth is that you have to earn it. In other words,

you have to give it for you to receive it – it is reciprocal. When you treat someone with respect, however hard headed they were when interacting with you, their opinion of you will begin to improve.

Rather than trying to label difficult people as being impossible, try to change your perspective of them. Always perceive them as an essential component of your team – one that the team cannot do without. It could be that they like challenging every idea, protocol, or project you initiate. When you make that shift in your mentality and perception of them, they will start to change how they talk about you. The point is for you to listen keenly to their feedback and then act accordingly.

Focus on what can be actioned

There are times when your awkward friends, colleagues, or family colleagues put you into a hot soup. For instance, you may have some work to be turned in, but then they fail to do it, or they may do something, and then you are held responsible for it when you don't even deserve that kind of unfair treatment. Whatever it is that the difficult people in your life do to you, the first step towards resolving the matter is for you to accept that it has already happened. Instead of crying over spilled milk, simply focus on what the next steps should be like.

What are some of the necessary steps to take in resolving the situation?

Create the change you want to see.

Ignore
If you have already tried all you could and still thought that nothing works, the other trick is for you to ignore everything. The best way you can treat someone difficult is to ignore them. You cannot possibly argue with yourself, right? They may try as much as they can to trigger you into being angry or acting up. However, when you ignore them, you simply cause them to stop because they are not getting the kind of reaction they are looking for. When you act up, you are giving them the satisfaction that they won, and

they will keep on poking until you break.

Think about it, have you done everything you could within your means to handle the situation responsibly? If so, then you have nothing else to give them. Simply get on with your life and try as much as you can not to interface with them unless necessary. If they play a central role in your daily work and it is standing in the way of your productivity, then you can choose to escalate this to the higher authorities to help you resolve the issue. This is often referred to as a trump card. You should not use this unless you have exhausted all other possible options.

In most cases, if you want to get to someone moving, you can do it by employing the top-down approach. You must exercise caution when using this option. Try not to use it every often lest your bosses begin to think that you cannot handle small issues independently. While this works, it is only to be used when all else is depleted. Trust me, I have used it, and it works like magic.

Employ kindness

I get it, when you are dealing with a difficult person in your life, your gut feeling is usually to be difficult as well. When someone is attacking you, the first thought you have is often to try and defend yourself. I have been there, done that. The problem is that when you do this, you get sucked up into a vacuum such that you don't even take a moment to slow down and just breath.

In almost every difficult situation, I have found myself in is that showing kindness goes a long way in helping one calm the case down. When two difficult people are hard on each other, the chances are that the whole situation tends to escalate to the extent that nothing can be accomplished.

However, when you choose to be kind, you will diffuse the whole situation so that you can get all that you want. This is one of the techniques that should be at the top of your list whenever you encounter a difficult person in your life.

Show compassion

If you have been in a problem before, then you know that you must deal with your issues. The truth is, we all have issues, and we tend to think that what we are going through is so harsh that no one can bear. However, if you sat down to listen to what other people are going through, you will simply take your baggage with you and shove it back into your backpack.

Well, I love that!

My point is, no one knows what it feels like to have another's problems. When you are dealing with someone difficult, this should be your principle – it could be that they are experiencing a very tough ordeal or an enormous problem that you wouldn't even be able to bear in part.

Often, when you choose to show a problematic person a little bit of compassion, they tend to respond positively. Several of us get stuck in our heads and lives that we don't even open our eyes to what the people around us might be experiencing. Your friend might just be looking for a little kindness. The next time you encounter someone difficult – whether at work, home, or elsewhere – show them some kindness, and you will be amazed at how that works magic.

Find something in common

When you are talking to someone for the very first time, what you will note is that sharing something in common with them often makes your connection stronger. Each one of us has been made in such a way that we desire to belong to a group. We are natural beings that want to have a strong sense of belonging.

When you meet someone, it always feels nice to know that you both went to the same college, even if during different years. Having something in common creates a form of kinship. My children are in high school now, and each time I met a parent that has children the age of mine or that our children attend the same schools, I feel like we have a parental connection.

Today, if you have someone difficult in your office, at home or elsewhere, try to establish something that you both share in common. This will go a long way in helping you get along with each other afterward.

Control what you can

There are things in life that we can control, and others out of our control. One thing that is important to note is that we must focus our attention on the things that we can control.

When you are trying to handle a difficult situation with a difficult person, you must start by thinking about what it is in that situation that is within your control. It could be that there is someone else you can deal with instead of that difficult person. That is the person that might just pave the way for you to do things right.

A few months ago, I was trying to work with the sales department on a novel initiative I was trying to bring to life in our company. One of the team members suggested that I should speak to a specific person to seek their help because that has been the tradition. When I first contacted the person, I did not get a response. I kept sending them emails after emails, left several voicemails, but still did not get a response. I finally got frustrated and resorted to speaking to other people in the department.

Several people in the sales department were willing to help with the project with so much joy. That was a difficult person that I managed to workaround. Today, you can do the same – control all that you can!

Look at yourself

The scripture in James 1:23-24 states, "For anyone who hears the word but does not carry it out is like a man who looks at his face in a mirror, 24 and after observing himself goes away and immediately forgets what he looks like...."

If you are going to deal with a difficult person, then you will have to know who you are first. Your focus should be on what you hold inside you. Is there something that you are doing or not doing that is standing in your way of dealing with a difficult person?

There are so many of us who know precisely what kind of people we are. We know that we are always in a good mood and are sociable. Every single day is a smooth one. There are instances where you may have lots of things racing through your mind – solving one problem after the other.

Even when you are having a conversation with a friend, your mind is probably elsewhere. You may come off as though you are condescending, abrupt, and short. It is this kind of attitude that can make someone that is already irritated to get upset quickly. How you choose to respond will determine whether you are adding salt to injury or quenching the fire.

Therefore, spend some time to reflect on how you interact with other people – especially the difficult ones – to ensure that you are not making the situation worse than it already may be.

Overcome Your Fear of Conflict

If there is a technique that I like the most when dealing with someone difficult is overcoming my fear of conflict. You cannot deal with a difficult person if all you do is run away from them. So many people are scared of stirring up strife and conflict with a difficult person, but what you need to realize is that the more you try to run, the more you are giving that person the power to walk all over you.

While the process of dealing with someone difficult in itself is challenging enough, the truth is that if you do not stand up to them and set boundaries, the situation will only get worse than it already is. Each one of us deserves to be treated with respect. Therefore, do not allow them to manage you less than that.

Don't get me wrong; I am not saying that you should intentionally stir up conflict. What is merely asking you to do is that in the event a difficult person treats you less than you deserve to be treated, stand up to them and confront them about the whole situation. Conflict does not mean that it has to be something terrible. In so many cases, it is a good thing – especially when it leads to a resolution of issues and brings to fruition what you desire most.

The bottom line is, if you look around you, you will not miss at least one difficult person. You cannot run away from them. The key is for you to communicate with them gracefully and peacefully so that you can both reach a consensus. It is better to "agree to disagree" so that you can both move past your selfish interests and live a happier life.

Chapter 8

Expert techniques to handle difficult people

Practice reflective listening

Have you ever been upset, and then someone comes in and tells you, "I understand," Did that ever make you feel better?

I didn't think so!

Well, one thing that is important to note is that using such kind of statements will not help you accomplish anything. Let us consider an instance where you have a client in your company. They tell you that they are frustrated because of the budget cuts and the fact that you are not willing to offer them discounts even though they have been your loyal clients for several years. How do you respond to that? Do you just tell them that you understand what they are going through?

The truth is that if you did tell them you understand, that conversation is probably never going to have a good ending.

If you are in such a tight spot with a difficult client, the first thing you should tell yourself is to practice reflective listening. In other words, try to put yourself in the other person's shoes. Understand what it is that they are saying by simply interpreting their body language and words. This will help you to respond by reflecting their thoughts and emotional feelings back to them.

Instead of telling them plainly that you understand, try something like - "So, if I get you correctly, you are saying that our pricing is too high that is becoming a barrier to your business, right? – and because of the tight budget you are working with and the fact that we are not offering discounts. Is that right?"

If you have understood what they are telling you, simply move on with your conversation.

However, if you have not yet understood what they are going through, ask them to give you more information so that you can understand their situation better. The trick here is for you to make them feel that you get where they are coming from and that you are concerned. They want to feel your empathy.

Try as much as you can to avoid making promises you know you might not be able to meet. The goal is to make the difficult person feel that they have been heard and that they are greatly valued.

Consider their affect heuristic

This simply refers to a mental shortcut. This plays a significant role in helping you make a quick and efficient decision based on your emotional feelings towards the other person, situation, and the place you are at. In simple terms, our choices are greatly influenced by our experiences and general outlook of the world around us. It is merely because of our bias.

The leading cause of the problem is that we are not objective in such situations, and facts do not matter that much. We choose to run every decision we make based on our mental software and then develop strong opinions based on that.

If the difficult person keeps having a different opinion and keeps asking you what you think is the catch, try not to respond rubbish them off by saying that we have to move on because of ABCD's. There is a chance that this person may be trapped in another information source, contract, or agreement with the previous vendor who failed to deliver what they had promised they would. Based on that very experience, they may be looking at you through the same lenses.

What you need to do is ask questions so that you fully understand what the root cause of the problem is. Some of the questions you can ask them so that they can relax and offer you insight as to why they are resistant include;

- I really would like to understand why you are a little skeptical about this. Would you tell me more?

- **Is there anything we can do to relieve your fears?**
- What can we do to help you feel comfortable enough so that we can all move forward?

When you ask such questions, you are allowing them to simply redirect their thoughts from thinking that you are not trustworthy in considering what is needed for the team to move forward and make progress.

Tap into the beginner's mind

The beginner's mind is often referred to like the Zen mind, and it serves as a strategy of approaching each situation as though you have no prior experience in it. Whenever you adopt this kind of thinking when dealing with a difficult person, every conversation you engage in is made with the "I don't know" mindset. This allows you to try as much as you cannot judge the other person or the situation.

This also goes a long way in helping you not to

live with the 'should' kind of thinking. "You should have thought of the budget before the year started. You should have read my email concerning the discount expirations. You should have known that I am a busy person and available only once in a week for consultations."

When you are addressing a difficult person, try not to use 'should' statements. They only set your mind on the defensive and get in the way of your productivity and conversation before it can even start.

The good thing with adopting the Zen mindset is that it allows you to let go of an expert mindset. While you may be an expert in your field or in what you do, you have to realize that you are not an expert when it comes to a difficult person or situation.

For instance, instead of saying things like "You said that you wanted to increase your sales by 30% by the end of the month and the kind of delays am seeing will not make this possible," choose to approach the conversation in a beginner's mindset. Try not to prejudge the other person. Forget what it is that they should have done and perceive the conversation you are both having as a puzzle that needs to be solved.

You can choose to say something like this instead "It seems to me like with these delays, we will not be able to reach our sales goals. But, let's explore strategies that will help us achieve the results that we are aiming for." If you keenly study this statement, you will realize that you are acknowledging the fact that there is a problem, but immediately starts moving in the direction of a possible solution.

Let go of fear
Again, you cannot be afraid of negative results to the point that you allow that to drive your reactions. It is because of doubt that we tend to feel the need to control things and the people around us. If a colleague is difficult, you may feel afraid of challenging them because that might just put your relationship at risk. If a client

expresses displeasure in your services, timelines, or pricing structure, you may be afraid because you think that you might not be able to fix the whole situation.

The first thing is to let go of the idea that there is something that needs fixing. When you are having a conversation with a difficult person – whether a friend, child, client, or coworker – remember that your role is to listen, understand what they are saying and then discern what the next steps forward should be. I don't mean that you start dishing out solutions immediately. Take time to go over what they have told you and then think through the possible solutions to find the best way forward.

For instance, rather than trying to validate emotional feelings, slap together common fixes, or apologizing, what you can do is express how unfortunate it is that the situation happened once again. Assure the other person that you get how the whole situation is affecting the business or your relationship and then appreciate them for being patient enough to allow you to work towards resolving the issue.

"Chunk" the problem

You may be wondering what 'chunking' is all about. Well, this simply refers to the process of taking a huge problem and then breaking it down into smaller manageable portions that you can address one at a time. When you break problems into smaller portions, this allows you to handle them. They also make people more willing to start dealing with all the issues at hand.

What I have learned from my mentor over the years is the importance of chunking things and then organizing them into tasks that you can handle every other day. This is the same way you can choose to deal with a tough situation with a difficult person.

Does your employee always find a reason not to turn in their work on time because they cannot get started using the new software?

What you can do is to ask them to help you break down each of the steps into smaller bite-size pieces that you can work on to come up with an easy to follow protocol. The point is for you not to apportion blame or say that they are lazy, but to find the best way forward. When each task is chunked, it becomes easier for the other person to digest what is left to be done.

Remember, anger is natural
We have all encountered difficult people – clients, friends, and colleagues alike – that we get so furious. It could also be that you have been on the other side of things. For instance, if you are a customer at a store and you pay for a new product upgrade, and then you realize that it is shallow that it makes you angry.

The recalibration theory of anger states that anger is a natural emotion that is wired into human beings. In other words, you have to realize that anger is the best way we have been made to get into the bargain. We press our lips together, bite our tongue, furrow our brows, or flare our nostrils just so that we can drive the other person to a place of higher value based on what we have to give.

If you are dealing with a difficult person, the point is for you to try and avoid justifying your actions or position. Realize that the reason why they could be feeling that way is that they think that their opinion is being undervalued or that they want to control the situation. It is advisable that you take the other person's frustrations seriously and not personally. Once you have understood the frustrations and arguments of the other person, thank them for bringing that to your attention. Also, let them know that you will think through everything and get back to them with a solution or a way forward.

When the other person is already furious, the chances are that they will not take any solution you offer at that time. However right the answer might be, they will not feel like it is the best way to go about the whole situation. Therefore, you must allow them some time to calm down before you can pick up the discussions where you left them – this time, with practicality and reason.

But what if the difficult person is already raging with anger, how can you deal with the situation?

Well, there are so many ways you can try to calm the whole situation down;

Keep your calm

This is probably a point you will see everywhere in this book – because it is essential and easy to get wrong. If someone sends you an angry text or email or starts shouting at you on the phone, the truth is that it is hard not to get personal. There is a chance that you will get a bristle of anger, and defensive thoughts will begin to pop into your mind of how wrong you think the other person is. You will start to think about how ungrateful they are for all the hard work you give the company, and before you know it, you are exploding with fury.

The best thing to do is to take in a deep breath. Try to take in what it is that the other person is trying to say. In between those lines, you might note that the other person is in a struggle or is frustrated with the whole process, product or service to the point that they took it out on you or the team. We are all human, and there are times when we are caught in our moments of weakness. If you try to understand this fact, you will not see the reason why you should take their difficulty, comments, or arguments personally or hold it against them.

If the other person is being abusive, rude, or aggressive in their language or intonation, don't tolerate their behavior. If, at some point during the conversation, you feel like they are belittling you, simply feel free to escalate the situation to a third-party that can help you resolve without killing the other.

Let us consider an instance where a client calls the support team in your company expressing how upset they are about the delay in the delivery of their products. They may be agitated and are shouting at the top of their lungs on the phone call. This is where your support team or you should remain calm and try to ask the three what's; what is the problem, what are their goals, needs or desires, and what are the available options. If you are the one on the other side of the phone, keep your cool and find out more details about their issue. That alone will work to de-escalate an angry person.

Practice active listening

Try as much as you can to focus on what they are saying - rather than the anger behind their words and voice. When your attention is on what they are really saying, you will be better placed to determine what it is that is agitating them. This will also help you resolve the issue rather than trying only to de-escalate it to comfort them. When you know what the problem is, you can find a solution, and you will have a satisfied colleague, friend, or client at the end of the day.

Let us consider an instance where a client walks into your store and tells you that the product you sold them stopped working for them a few days after they bought it. They continue to tell you how surprised and disappointed that you could offer such a poorly designed product.

What will you do? What will your response be like?

Well, the simplest way to go is to pay attention to the words they use – surprised, disappointed. Those are the words they used to express their emotional feelings. The point is that they are not angry but surprised by how your product behaved.

In such an instance, you may be tempted to respond with the words "I understand that you are frustrated..." while that is a response, it is not only going to escalate the other person's feelings but will now make them angry. By saying that, you are only giving them a reason to go from disappointment and surprise to anger.

However, if you demonstrate that you are actively listening to what they have to say, you will calm the situation down. You can say things like "that is certainly surprising and disappointing. Let me take a look to know why the product stopped working unexpectedly." With this response, you are acknowledging the client's feelings without necessarily escalating them.

Repeat back what your customers say

One of the key components of active listening is ensuring that your client and you are on the same page. Once you know the root cause of their anger, you can simply repeat what you heard from them so that you are sure you understand what is making them angry. In so doing, you are also letting the other person know that you get hat their concerns are and are working on a resolution or response.

Let us consider an instance where someone badges into your office ranting about the product you sold them not working. You can simply start your response with such words as "What am hearing you say is…" this will simply get the ball rolling. Try to highlight how the issue is standing in the way of them achieving their goals. This will show them that you did not just listen but understood their needs and are going to help them.

Thank them for bringing the issue to your attention

When the other person you are conversing with is angry and is sending negative vibes about the whole situation, you can thank them for speaking out their concerns. This will go a long way in helping you establish a good rapport with them. With just a simple 'thank you,' acknowledging their time and contributions, you will sufficiently calm the situation down.

One of the best ways you can deal with someone who is continuously difficult and angry is to ensure that you thank them each time. When a difficult member of your team starts an inquiry, simply acknowledge their efforts for reaching out. If you have held onto a case file for extended durations of time, thank your team for being patient while you were troubleshooting. When that difficult person shares their negative views about the project, thank them for being bold enough to share their perspective and making the whole team better.

Explain the steps you'll take to solve the problem
When that difficult person at your office raises an issue, you must make it clear to them that you will get started on addressing their concerns. It does not matter whether or not it is a simple issue that you can finish up over the phone or something that requires a whole process that might take days, weeks or even months – the trick is for you to plainly and spell out your intentions and next moves to them so that they feel valued, heard and at ease.

One of the best ways you can achieve this is if you set timelines for their issue to be sorted out. Spell out every single step you intend to take, and when each one of the steps is expected to be complete. This way, you are communicating to the other person that you know exactly what it is that you are doing and the time when you expect to have a resolution ready.

Set a time to follow-up with them, if needed

There are instances when a simple phone conversation cannot resolve the problems that arise between you and another person. Some will require you to sync up with the manager or fill up a request form for the resolution process to be initiated. If that is the case in your instance, then you will need to explain this to the other person. Try to give them timelines of when you expect to have a response for them.

The benefit of talking directly to the other person is so that your client, coworker, or friend has ample time to calm down. At the same time, this will give you sufficient time to seek guidance and feedback from your superiors on how best to proceed. If at all, you will need to follow up with the other person, explain clearly why that break would greatly benefit them.

For instance, it could be that you will need to speak to the product expert for troubleshooting purposes. The point is that you are as transparent with them as possible. Let them stay aware that they cannot take any further action, at least until you can seek clarification with those concerned as well.

If they keep being uneasy about what you propose to them, you can also choose to offer them a contingency plan. Tell them exactly when they expect you to reach out to them and the kind of information you will have for them. This will justify the follow up you will be taking up with them.

Be sincere

The same way remaining calm when dealing with a difficult person is essential, so is sincerity. Trust me, people know when they are being spoken to in a somewhat condescending way or even an angry manner. Choose the right set of words to use and the intonation to employ when communicating with a difficult person. Ensure that your tonal voice is not only intentional but also respectful. No one likes being talked to with an angry tone. Simply take the high road and make the other person feel like what they are saying is being taken seriously.

There are times when that difficult person in your office will call you at midnight with an "issue," but then after reading through or troubleshooting, you realize that it was an error on their part. You may be tempted to poke fun on the other person who did not pay attention enough to pick the error out, costing you your good night's sleep.

What you need to understand is that this other person could very well be you. It is through them that you know whether the services you render are quality enough or not. Even though they may be at fault, it is their contribution that makes the whole product quality. Therefore, ensure that you are politely explaining the reason why an issue arose in the first place and the best ways to prevent them from happening in the future again.

Highlight the case's priority

One of the common frustrations for people who conflict is feeling like their support case is not as crucial to the business as the other person's. This is especially the case when dealing with a company or a situation that has a broader client coverage. The other person might feel as though their case is expendable while the rest of the team is busy providing poor experiences.

To get this feeling out of the way, you must highlight how critical the situation is to everyone involved - whether directly or indirectly. Let the other person know that you are putting in efforts to notify essential stakeholders in the company so that the issue they are concerned about is resolved as fast as possible. This way, they will feel as though the whole company is on their case even if it's only one support team that is working on it.

One last word

Indeed, dealing with difficult people is one of the toughest tasks in life. They are the kind of people who will ruin your perfect day before it can even begin. It could be a colleague, family member, partner, or friend. It could also be anyone random you run into at the street. Whoever that may be, the trick is to ensure that you have armed yourself with the above methods, steps, and approaches to deal with them appropriately.

Realize that difficult people exist all around us, and if you don't do something about them, then you risk letting them hurt others.

The truth is that there is no easy way to deal with these people – after all, they are different combinations of personality traits. They all have different ways to make others' life difficult.

As the saying goes, "It takes two to tango." Realize that these difficult people may not even notice that they are difficult. To most of them, this is their usual way of life. In fact, to a difficult person, everyone else around them is difficult. They don't have your perspective of things.

So, have you been continually dealing with difficult people yourself? If so, it might be time for you to take a look at your behavior. Ask yourself whether you are the one being difficult. Look for such indicators as;

- **Lack of close connections at home, school or the workplace**
- You lack a sense of self-worth in what you do
- **You find yourself being misunderstood too often or complaining about this or that**
- You always think that people are talking ill of you
- **You still are an emotional person**
- You feel like people don't even care or remember you

You might just be the difficult person we have been discussing here. If that is the case, then it is high time you use the strategies above to deal with your behavior. If these traits are what you see in someone around you, then you can also use the techniques we have discussed to help them become a better person.

Remember, a little self-reflection goes a long way in helping us be a better person to the people working and interacting with us daily.

You can help yourself and the difficult person around you to see what they are doing so that they can change for the long-term.

It is a win for all of us!

So, what are you waiting for? Start identifying them around you and help them BECOME!

© Written by:Katerina Griffith

Made in the USA
Middletown, DE
07 May 2020

94080075R10089